Eight Months' Experience

OF

THE SEPOY REVOLT,

IN 1857,

BY

Major-Gen. Sir Charles D'Oyly, Bart.,

LATE BENGAL STAFF CORPS.

———o———

Eight Months' Experience

OF

THE SEPOY REVOLT,

IN 1857,

BY

Major-Gen. Sir Charles D'Oyly, Bart.,

LATE BENGAL STAFF CORPS.

The Naval & Military Press Ltd

Published by
The Naval & Military Press Ltd

The Naval & Military Press

MILITARY HISTORY AT YOUR FINGERTIPS

... a unique and expanding series of reference works

Working in collaboration with the foremost regiments and institutions, as well as acknowledged experts in their field, N&MP have assembled a formidable array of titles including technologically advanced CD-ROMs and facsimile reprints of impossible-to-find rarities.

EIGHT MONTHS' EXPERIENCE

OF THE

SEPOY REVOLT IN 1857.

―――――o―――――

CHAPTER I.

Outbreak of the Mutiny—Causes assigned—Emeute at Barrackpore—My duties at the Haupper Stud—Mutiny at Meerut on the 10th May—Our flight from Haupper—Scenes at Meerut—Return to Haupper—Organize Native Police—Threatened with attack from Walidad Khan, of Maligurh—Mutinous conduct of our Treasure Guard—Second flight into Meerut.

―――――o―――――

The first mutterings of the storm which burst in all its fury on British India, 1857, were heard in the early part of that year. It took shape in the military revolt of the Bengal Native Army, which shook to its centre the prestige and even the very existence of the British power in the East, and terminated in the complete and total defeat of the mutinous troops and the subsequent reconstruction of the Government of the country on a more secure basis.

It is not my intention at this time to enter at large upon the causes which led up to the Mutiny; suffice it is to say, that the causes were numerous, all conducing more or less to the result, some of which I will briefly touch upon.

There can be no doubt that for some time previous to the year 1857 an uneasy feeling had been springing up in the ranks of the native troops. There had been indications of an insubordinate spirit, which it had been found necessary to suppress. Sir Charles Napier when Commander-in-Chief in India found occasion to disband the 66th B. Native Infantry for refusing to march on service, only two or three years before. It must moreover be borne in mind that the British Government, by successive conquests. had extended its sway considerably; that after thet otal overthrow and extinction of the Khalsa Army in the Punjab, in 1848-1849, there was no state on the continent of India of sufficient power to cope with the British Forces; that certain States had lapsed to the Government, through the absence of accredited heirs to the Throne ; and that all these extensions and acquisitions were made, without any corresponding addition being made to the English portion of the Army. That the Native portion in great part were recruited from the high caste Brahman, thus constituting a powerful hierarchy which proved a dangerous element at critical times. It is also alleged by certain writers that the annexation of Oude, in 1855, from which many of our recruits were drawn, exercised considerable influence on the Mutiny of 1857. I do not, myself, attach much importance to the last reason assigned, but I readily admit that once the revolt had broken out, the annexation of Oude then became a dominant factor in the support of the rebellion. Unquestionably, the paucity of English Troops in India, compared with the vast extent of territory to be governed, was a powerful operating cause. In 1857 there was only one European Regiment stationed between Calcutta and Allahabad, a distance of some 800 miles. It was oblvious to the instigators of the rebellion that, under these circumstances, any emeute of the Native Army must have good hopes of success. It only required the light to the train to secure it. The unfortunate incident of the greased cartridges afforded the immediate pretext for revolt. A new cartridge had been introduced into the Army, which, for its efficient use, required grease to lubricate it. Although pains were taken to prove to the Sepoys that the purest grease was used in the Arsenals for the manufacture of these cartridges, in order not to offend their religious feelings, which were highly sensitive on the point, reports were disseminated among all ranks that the Government had determined upon breaking the caste of the Hindoo soldier by the use of cows' fat, and of the Mahomedan by the use of pigs' fat. It was useless to combat this unfounded rumour. The more it was contradicted, the more the evil report spread, and I unhesitatingly affirm my belief that more than two-thirds of the Native Army gave credit to it.

At Barrackpore, a large Military Station near Calcutta, an emeute arising from this cause took place on the parade ground, early in 1857, where the Sepoys refused to obey the orders of their officers. This was promptly suppressed at the time by General Hearsay, and the Adjutant of the Regiment, who shot down the offending soldier, and the revolt ceased for a time, only to break out with fresh vigour at Meerut, on the 10th of May.

At that time I was a Captain in charge of a large and important depôt of horses for the Army, numbering some 2,000 colts, with an establishment of a European officer, as an assistant, a Veterinary Surgeon, four Sergeants, from Cavalry and Artillery Regiments, as Overseers, three Office Writers, besides a large Native Establishment. All the European Officers and Sergeants were married men, and most of them had families. I was living in a large house, well furnished, with a beautiful park surrounding it, with horses, carriages, and all the comforts of life. A few weeks afterwards found me a fugitive, with simply the clothes I stood in, bereft of wife, furniture and property. But I am anticipating. At the time I refer to, viz., the beginning of May, I was busily employed in getting in my yearly supply of oat straw. I took my early rides to inspect the Depôt Farm, carried out my daily course of duty, with my evening drive in the phæton, and everything seemed calm and quiet, and likely to remain so.

I had occasion to visit the weighments of the straw, where I employed to assist me (to whom I gave extra pay for the work) some intelligent Native Officers and men, attached to the guard over the Treasure Chest. I spoke to them on the subject of the greased cartridges and asked them if they thought it possible that the Government had conceived the idea of breaking their caste by using the fat which was interdicted by their religion. They replied that "individually they did not think so, but that everyone was saying that it was so, and that it was difficult to know what to believe or to disbelieve" I told them that the reports were lying rumours, and begged them not give credit to them, but I was convinced from the manner of their reply that they thought there was more foundation for the rumour than I was inclined to admit. They were, however, most respectful and certainly did not show the slightest symptoms of an inclinaion to mutiny. I find in a letter written to my Commanding Officer, Major Thatcher, dated the 26th April, 1857, the following words—"What a state they are in at Calcutta about the Mutineers. I have been talking to the *Havildar of the Guard here. They are not yet affected with the mutinous spirit, so I need not fear for my Treasury."

On the 10th of May we heard some heavy firing in the direction of Meerut, one of the largest military stations in the N.W. Provinces. The garrison consisted of Artillery, Horse and Foot. (Meerut was the head-quarters of the Bengal Artillery) the 60th Royal Rifles, the 6th Dragoon Guards, (the Carabineers) two Native Infantry Regiments, besides details of Sappers, &c. On the morning of the 11th we were startled by seeing some Native Cavalry horses, galloping about the Depot without riders, and covered with gashes from sword cuts. They were caught and stabled. In the course of the evening a messenger brought me a note from Major Thatcher, who was then in Meerut, informing me that that the Native Troops, Horse and Foot, had mutinied, shot their officers and were off to Delhi; that I was at once to take measures to secure the safety of the Europeans at the Depot and advised flight to Futteygurh, or elsewhere down country. It is fortunate we did not follow this advice, for we should certainly have fallen into the hands of the rebels and as certainly have been murdered.

I took the note and consulted with Captain Parrott, my assistant, and we decided upon making the attempt to rush into Meerut, a distance of 22 miles, although the roads were covered

*A Havildar answers to a Non-Commissioned Officer in our Army.

with rebel soldiery and the villages *en route* swarming with armed ruffians. We sent out secret orders that the European portion of the establishment were to assemble just outside the Depot on the Meerut road, at 8.30 p.m. We made a few hasty arrangements for our flight by putting together some changes of linen, refreshment for ourselves, milk for the baby, &c., ordered the carriage and prepared to start. It was a moonlight night, which proved disadvantageous to us as we could be clearly distinguished, and form a mark for the rebels' fire-arms. At this juncture an unfortunate incident occurred. I had informed the Native Officer of my Treasure Guard, which was close to my house, that I was going into Meerut with my family for a few days, and then hoped to return. The carriage contained my wife and child (now Mrs. Bernard, then an infant of a year old) a native nurse, the coachman and myself. The Coachman who was a Mahomedan, at the last moment absented himself, purposely as I afterwards learned, and whilst we were waiting for him, the soldiers of the guard, suspecting that something was up, crowded round the carriage and one took hold of the horses' reins. I had a pair of spirited grey Arabs, who were not inclined to stand any rough usage. I shouted to the man to let go the bridle, whipped up the horses, who began to rear and jump into their collars, and so dashed off. I called out that I should soon be back with them, and in this manner bade adieu to Haupper, some of us never to return. We found the rest of the party assembled at the bridge, and forming a strongish cavalcade started on our flight at a quiet trot. The Sergeants rode their own horses, Captain Parrott and myself in our respective carriages, and the Veterinary Surgeon, a Mr. Burgess-Parry, a Dorsetshire man and fellow countyman, mounted on a grey Arab of mine, a noted horse on the Madras turf, called Prime Minister.

We reached the town of Haupper, the city from which the Depot derives its name, in two miles. Here we changed our tactics, and on a given signal we galloped as hard as we could through the town, till we arrived at the open country, on the grand trunk road to Meerut. The rush was so sudden and unexpected that we passed unchallenged, though we heard after we had passed, the discharge of fire-arms, which, however, proved harmless.

At early dawn, as we neared the city of Meerut, we were suddenly stopped by the challenge—" Who goes there ?" As we did not immediately answer, being taken by surprise, we narrowly escaped having a discharge of grape-shot into us from a couple of our Artillery guns, commanded by a Captain Minto. We quickly explained the cause of our appearance, and were then warmly welcomed by the rough Troopers of the Battery, who cheered us and congratulated us on our escape. We reached Meerut, two miles further, in safety, and having deposited the ladies and children in a fortified entrenchment, called the " Dum-dumma," I sallied forth to report my arrival to the General Officer, commanding the Troops.

In crossing the large open parade ground, adjacent to the Barracks, I met an officer in uniform whose face I seemed to know. As he neared me he put up his eye-glass, for he was short-sighted, and I immediately recognised a dear old friend, who had been a fellow cadet with me at the Military College, at Addiscombe, Edward Fraser, of the Engineers, a brother of the late Dr. Fraser, Bishop of Manchester. After fraternising I said—" My dear Ned, what are you doing here ? " He replied— " I have just arrived with a Native Company of Sappers, from Roorkee on our way to Delhi." He continued—" I have just been reporting the arrival of myself and company to General Hewett, commanding the Station." After a few more words we parted, and I never saw him again alive. On my return from reporting myself to the General I was re-crossing the parade ground, when I observed a party of soldiers carrying something heavy. I approached and to my horror ascertained that they were carrying a dead body. On lifting the cloth, that covered the face, I recognised the handsome features of my friend Edward Fraser, with whom I had been conversing only a little before, in perfect health and rejoicing in the prospects of service in the field. He had just been shot by his own men, under the mistaken impression that he had been to the General to organise an attack upon them by the European Troops. About half-an-hour afterwards we heard the sound of field guns, and were told that Captain Light of the Artillery, with two guns, was in pursuit of the Sappers, who had dispersed and taken to flight after the murder of poor Fraser, and the non-commissioned officers to the Company.

On my reaching the Barrack, in which General Hewitt had taken up his quarters, a striking and interesting scene presented itself to view. A native butcher, who had been prominent in the massacre of an officers' wife, on the day the mutiny broke out, had just been tried by a drum-head Court Martial and sentenced to be hung. The scene formed an impressive and remarkable tableau. A large Barrack-room, turned for the occasion into a Military Court of Law; Officers in various uniforms standing about; the President of the Court, still seated in his chair, with Brigade Major, Judge Advocate, and other members of the Staff around, having just concluded their Court Martial duties; at the end of the room the prisoner, an ill-looking Mahomedan, standing guarded by an Artilleryman, with arm bared to the elbow and holding his bayonet within an inch of the culprit's body, every muscle quivering with excitement, as if he longed to put an end to the murderer's life on the spot, by plunging the instrument into his heart. The light from an upper window fell on the two figures and intensified the effect, the rest of the room being cast into shadow, from the jalousies being closed to keep out the scorching rays of the terrific May sun. The subject would have formed a grand tableau for the painter, and the powerful impression it left on my mind will never fade from memory.

I returned to the Fort, found it crowded with fugitives from all the surrounding stations, and most uncomfortable for ladies and children in such terribly hot weather. I fortunately fell in with General Harriott, of the Judge Advocate General's Department, who kindly insisted on my wife and child and nurse taking refuge in his comfortable house, not far removed from the fort. There was certainly the chance of some rebel soldiery, or ill disposed marauder, attacking us, when removed from the immediate precincts of our own troops. On the other hand, considering my wife and child were both unwell from the effects of the night's adventure and likewise that the great body of the mutineers had gone clean off to Delhi, I chose, as I thought, the least of two evils and decided upon accepting the kind offer of the General and took them to the house. My wife was taken dangerously ill that night I will not dwell upon the terrible sorrow which fell upon me, in addition to my other troubles· Within 24 hours from that time I had lost and laid in her last home, with her newly born babe by her side, the partner of my life, who had acted so bravely and with such heroic courage through the scenes I have just described, and I was left a widower with a young child to provide for and face with as brave a heart as I could command, but with a broken spirit the terrible prospect which was opening before us.

The funeral over, and my baby left in the charge of a kind hearted lady, who offered to befriend her, I decided upon returning to my post at Haupper. I was dissuaded by my friends from undertaking this (what I may term) perilous duty, and as I was told by one kind friend that I was a d—— fool for attempting it. But after the domestic loss I had suffered, my feelings were callous to danger and I rode back alone with what feelings you may imagine, to throw myself into the hands of a mutinous soldiery, sorrow stricken, depressed, weary in body and harassed in mind, to meet a future which foreshadowed the direst trouble to me individually, and possible ruin to the British power in India. I rode into my grounds exhausted; was immediately surrounded by Sepoys, who, to my surprise and pleasure, helped me off my horse, placed me on a wicker couch, offered me shirbet and cakes, and condoled with me in the most touching way on the great affliction I had suffered, and brought to my mind many little acts of kindness which my wife had been able to do for some of the young soldiers, who had formed part of our escort, during the last cold weather tour.

Thus ended my first flight from Haupper, to be repeated on two occasions as shall hereafter be told. On my return to the Depot I was rejoiced to find my Commanding Officer, Major Thatcher, had taken up his quarters in my house. He had come there from Meerut, hearing of my affliction, to share my danger and responsibilities at all risks, a kind and gallant act which I here acknowledge with deep gratitude.

We thus found ourselves the only two Europeans to conduct the duties of this vast establishment But the native subordinates worked well, the Sepoys appeared fairly well disposed, were pleased to see us amongst them, and we set to work to carry out as best we could the onerous duties which fell to our unassisted hands. It occured to us, while talking over the situation, that the contingency of the Sepoy Guard rising in mutiny and carrying off the Treasure to Delhi, was always on the cards, and that it would be wise to provide against it. It must be borne in mind that Delhi was the objective point to which the native mind and eyes were attracted. The Mutineers had set up the puppet King of Delhi as their chief and head of the rebellion. He lived there in the Palace, whither flocked to join his standard all the mutinous Army, and, in addition, all the disaffected rogues and ruffians in the country; an innumerable host of the seething scum of the populous towns gathered together to see what plunder and profit to themselves might be picked up, during the anarchy and confusion consequent on the outbreak.

It is beyond the scope of this paper to enter upon the military movements made on our part to re-capture the city, and restore tranquility to the country at large. But the varying fortunes of our arms, and the delay which occured in massing a sufficient body of troops to besiege the city, made a marked impression on the behaviour and conduct, not only of the neighbouring petty chiefs, but likewise of the more orderly portion of the agricultural community, and particularly of the more lawless and predatory class. The population in the neighbourhood of my Depot was composed chiefly of Jats, a fine body of peasantry, deriving their name, I believe, from the old stock of Jhut Sikhs. They were, on the whole, a well conducted body of men, some of them given to petty pilfering and cattle lifting and other misdemeanours of a like nature, but not addicted to more serious crimes. Another portion of the community was composed of Goojurs, a very inferior class, thieves by profession and practice, and at perpetual enmity with the Jats above mentioned.

It occured to us that if we could raise a Police composed of Jats, it might serve to keep in check any attempt of the Native Guard to mutiny, and likewise awe the Goojurs from attempting the plunder of the Government property under our charge With this object in view, Major Thatcher applied to the Brigade Major at Meerut to supply us with as many muskets as could be spared. The application was favourably received, and we obtained some 80 to 100 stands of muskets, with ammunition. Thus provided with arms, we sent for Jumayut Sing, an old Jat. He was the chief of the robbers in the N. W. Provinces, a fine old man of undeniable courage and full of resource.

It was the custom in those days for the Government to pay black mail to him, for the protection of the Depot and its surroundings. If any cattle were lifted, as was occasionally the case, Jumayut Sing was bound to make good the loss. He knew the names and whereabouts of all the robbers in the country, and could recover stolen cattle in places where it would be impossible for us to do so. To this man we had recourse and ordered him to raise 100 men for police purposes, whom we armed with the muskets obtained from Meerut.

To the moralist, and what I may call the straight laced pedant, it may appear a lax system of ethics to make use of such questionable tools, but in times of danger to the State, the Government servant is bound to use all practicable means, provided they are not absolutely unjustifiable, to attain the object of protecting his charge, and acting on the principle that "all is fair in love and war," we utilised the services of this reputed bandit and never regretted doing so.

I may here mention in passing, that in after years when I was Deputy Superintendent I did away with what I considered the objectionable practise of black mail, and obtained in substitution the services of the Police; and I may further add that poor old Jumayut Sing, who always proved loyal to me and did good service for the Government during those times, was some years afterwards killed in a Dacoity or burglary, in which he was the head agent.

In this way we organised a rough Police. We discovered an old cannon, which had been hidden for ages, buried in a neighbouring village. This we unearthed and placed it on a platform, raised on a mound of earth, commanding the road to the Depot. I should have been sorry to have been ordered to fire it off, as it would most certainly have burst, being crenalated and worn out. But it served its purpose, for the rumour went forth through the country that the English Officers had formed a battery of guns, so that none but regular troops had better attempt an attack.

At this time our attention was much taken up by the conduct of the Treasure Guard. They were a detail of the 20th Regiment, Native Infantry, which had commenced the mutiny on the 10th of May, at Meerut, had shot their officers, Captains Taylor and MacDonald, Lieutenants Henderson and Pattle, on the parade ground, besides women and children. Their bearing became daily more insolent and their behaviour suspicious. I speak of the ring-leaders amongst them, and the ill disposed, for there were some young soldiers who kept us duly acquainted with the intentions and actions of their comrades. These young soldiers told us that, the Regiment to which they belonged, after their arrival at Delhi, had written to them to shoot their officers (meaning us) and to join them with the treasure they were guarding at Haupper.

One day a young soldier walked into my dining-room and said—" Sahib, I have brought you some cardamums, put them into your drinking water, you will find them cool it." There were some of my servants in the room at the time he entered, so, under some pretext, I took him into another room apart and asked him the purport of his visit, as I knew very well he had something on his mind, besides cardamums. He replied—" For God's sake do not allow Major Thatcher, or go yourself, amongst the Guard. They are only waiting an opportunity to shoot you and take away the treasure to Delhi. I thanked him and assured him that we would be careful and take precautions. But to do this was a matter of difficulty. That evening, at dinner-time, Major Thatcher rose, closed the door behind us, (they were open to admit a free current of air in the hot weather) and on my remonstrating, he remarked—" It is a precaution against having a volley of bullets fired into us while we are at dinner." His action was too practical and wise for further opposition, but the circumstance took off my appetite for the meal, and we went to bed with nerves somewhat shaken and spirits depressed.

About 20 miles to the eastward, a little off the main road to the civil station of Boolund-shur, there was the fort of Malaghur, held by a chief named Walidad Khan. This man, on the King of Delhi being proclaimed ruler of the country by the rebel Army, immediately cast off his allegiance to the British Government, threw in his lot with the King of Delhi, and promised him his fealty and assistance I received from him, one day, a most impertinent letter, informing me that the King of Delhi was now ruler of the country ; that the English authorities had been deposed, and cooly added that he proposed to come over with his troops to take possession of the Depot, in the name of the King. I knew there was little hope of receiving assistance from the Meerut authorities, as I had already applied for a European Guard, but was refused on the score that not an English soldier could be spared from the station. We therefore sent for Jumayut Sing, the head of the robbers, and explained to him the situation I read him the letter I had received from Walidad Khan and consulted him as to future action. As I stated before, this man was a Jat by caste, and it was handed down by tradition among his people that the country now held by the British had formerly belonged to them. His reasoning, therefore, was plain and practical. He argued—" If the English are driven out of the country, as a matter of course, the land belongs to us, and not to such men as Walidad Khan, or any other Mahomedan usurper." So after pulling his grey beard, and reflecting for a few moments he said—" D'Oyly sahib, there is no cause for alarm. I will send out scouts to Malagurh, who shall report to me every movement of this villain ; not a man shall leave the Fort without my being made aware of it, and if they should come in force, I will have the Dhools, or big drums, sounding in the neighbouring villages. This will collect about 1000 young men to bar their entry into the Depot."

These were big words, and, although the old man was excited, he meant all he said. He continued—" D'Oyly sahib, write him back a bold letter ; tell him to come and try it on, and if he should attempt it, we will then give him a sound dressing." Major Thatcher and I concocted a letter to the above effect and waited the result.

When we retired to rest on the evening mentioned a little before, it was not to take off our clothes and lie down between the comfortable sheets, but to take such rest as we could procure in our day clothes, with swords handy and pistols under the pillow, ready in a moment to spring up in defence of life. It was about two o'clock when I was awaked from fitful sleep by the sound of Cavalry on the gravel walk outside. Major Thatcher slept on the verandah, it being cooler ; I slept in an inner room. I jumped up hastily, thinking it was Walidad's horsemen come to attack us, having given the go-by to Jumayut Sing's watchmen. I put my pistol into my belt and clutched my sword. And here a ludicrous incident occured. In fastening on my sword, the hook caught in the pillow case, and I ran rushing out to see what was the matter, with the pillow case and pillow dangling about my hips. It was no laughing matter then, but the recital of the story in later years has often caused amusement.

I found Major Thatcher, standing in the verandah, with pistol in hand confronting the Cavalry. We heard the command in English—" Front form threes," then " Dismount." Major Thatcher called out " Who are you ? and where do you come from ? " The answer was—" We come from Meerut by the General's orders, with a letter from Major Waterfield, the Brigade Major. Major Thatcher said—" Throw it to me." The Native Officer threw the letter, which ran thus—" Dear Bob, I send you a detachment of the 3rd Light Cavalry. They will be under your orders. They are sent to assist you." Major Thatcher turned to me—" Good Heavens! we are done for! These fellows will collude with the Infantry and off to Delhi with the Treasure to-morrow. What is to be done ? "

After a few minutes' reflection, a happy thought struck us. We called the Native Officer of the Cavalry and said—" You have been sent here to take our Treasure into Meerut." He replied—" He had no cart for the purpose." Again a bright thought came to our relief. We said—" There is no occasion for a cart, the troopers will take the pistols out of their holsters, carry them elsewhere and place the money in their holster pipes." There was a sum of about 18,000 rupees in silver, but how to manage for bags in which to place the money. The question was solved thus—We went to my wardrobe, where I had my linen, dozens of white socks and pocket handkerchiefs. We filled them with rupees, tied up the ends ; reserved a certain sum to pay the Native Infantry Guard, and gave the rest to the troopers to carry into Meerut, with a note to the Brigade Major telling him what we had done. For my part I never expected the bullion to reach its destination, but our plan succeeded, and we got receipt for the money.

Having started off the Cavalry with the money, it being then day-break, we called the Native Officers of the Infantry Guard, told them that the bulk of the treasure had been taken by the Cavalry into Meerut; that their services were, therefore, no longer required ; that they had acted like good soldiers in remaining faithful to their trust; that we should give them their arrears of pay, with three months' pay in advance, besides a gratuity, and certificates of good behaviour; that they might take away their fire-arms, (we could not prevent their taking them so made a virtue of necessity) advised them to go to their homes, and when the rebellion was over to rejoin the colours, when they would be rewarded and probably promoted, I must confess that the gratuity and promises were beyond their deserts, as we knew that some of them had not been faithful at heart, but to all outward seeming they had behaved well, and it was somewhat under pressure and actuated by expediency that we treated them as we did.

Major Thatcher then handed the pay to the native officer for distribution to the men. Meanwhile I had ordered our horses to be saddled and brought round to the back of the house to the bath-room door. While Major Thatcher was talking to the Native Officer, I peeped out to see what was going on outside with the Guard, found them in a state of great excitement and putting on their accoutrements. The position looked so threatening that I returned, took Major Thatcher aside, whispered to him that mischief was brewing amongst the Sepoys and that we must be off at once, or we should be shot. We slipped out, mounted our horses, and were off across the fields to Meerut, expecting every moment to hear bullets whizzing by us; but our departure was so quiet and sudden that we took them by surprise and were soon out of danger. Within an hour of our leaving the Depot the whole party, with one exception, were on the road to Delhi, distant 28 miles, and the Native Officers were both of them (we afterwards learned) killed during the siege.

CHAPTER II.

Return to Haupper—Attack on Walidad Khan's Picquet—Arrival of the mutinous Rohilcund Brigade—Measures taken to save the young Stock and third flight into Meerut—Night march with Escort—Take a Trooper into Meerut as Prisoner—Court Martial and Sentence.

————o————

On return to Meerut I went to Captain Johnson's (now Sir Edwin Johnson) house in the Artillery lines, but after a few days, hearing that all was quiet at the Depot after the departure of the Sepoys, I retraced my steps on the 16th of June to resume my duties there. On arrival I found four or five officers in my house. Captain Charles Gough, now Sir Charles Gough, V.C., and his brother Hugh, now Sir Hugh Gough, V.C., commanding a division in India, Captain Tyrwhitt, now General Tyrwhitt, of the Irregular Cavalry, a Mr. Lyall, of the Civil Service, now Sir Alfred Lyall, late Governor of the N. W. Provinces, and now a member of the Indian Council, then lately come out from Haileybury and Eton, a gallant and very promising officer, and another young officer, whose name I now forget. They were expecting to be attacked by Walidad Khan, mentioned before, who taking our inaction for pusillanimity was daily becoming bolder, and had thrown out a picquet within eight or nine miles of the Depot. He had three guns, had stopped the Government posts and was levying taxes on the neighbouring country. As this aggressive conduct was becoming intolerable, we again applied to Meerut for European troops. They sent us two field guns, under Captain T. P. Smith, (familiarly known as Tippy Smith), a cheery good fellow, 40 of H.M. 60th Rifles, under Captain Mortimer, a troop of the 6th Dragoon Guards, (the Carabineers) under Captain Wardlaw, with Lieut. Baker Russell as subaltern, now Sir Baker Russell, a distinguished soldier and noted Cavalry leader. The whole force under command of Major

Thatcher, of the Stud Department. To this small force was added some 60 troopers of the Irregular Cavalry, under Captain Tyrwhitt. We marched at 2 p.m., on a dark night, and came on the enemy's position at 6 a.m., but they had made a precipitate flight on hearing of our approach. The Cavalry and Artillery were, therefore, sent on in pursuit. We overtook a party of their rear guard, whom we charged : as we neared them, one man levelled his musket at me, but fortunately missed, and I dropped him with a ball from my pistol. We killed about 20 of them. The pursuit was under a fearful sun on the 18th of June; no rain had fallen for months and the heat was deadly. We stopped our pursuit when close to the Fort of Malaghur, for, having only two field guns, we could do nothing more, so halted and returned to rejoin the Infantry. We obtained some water to drink from the village, but it was dirty and full of living creatures. We were so parched with thirst that we were forced to drink some of it, till some villager brought a number of water melons. What a rush there was for the fruit! and oh! the rapture of swallowing the delicious morsels! In consequence of the over-powering heat, one gunner dropped down from sun stroke, five more were taken ill during the day, and the horses (one dropped down dead in his traces) were completely knocked up.

We had been in the saddle some 14 hours, great part of the time under a burning sun, and were glad to get back to my house. That evening, at dinner-time, I was told that a messenger was outside wishing to see me. I went out and recognised one of our scouts, who informed me that the whole of the Rohilcund Brigade, composed of Native Artillery and Cavalry and Infantry, had arrived at Ghurmuptesir Ghaut, on the Ganges, about 16 miles distant, and were preparing to cross over to our side of the river. Their route to Delhi, lay directly through my Depot.

This Rohilcund Brigade, which garrisoned the stations of Bareilly, Moradabad, and Shahjehanpore, had recently mutinied, shot many of their officers, besides women and children, and committed other atrocities. At Shahjehanpore they attacked the residents, while they were at Church, and massacred a number of them. But a good many of the residents of these stations had escaped to the hills, and placed themselves under the protection of native chiefs, or well disposed members of the native community. An interesting account of the Rohilcund mutiny was written by Mr. Cracroft Wilson, the Commissioner of the District.

On hearing the report mentioned above, I instantly sent off a messenger, on a camel, to the officer commanding the troops that had just left us, to beg him to return with his force and offer resistance to the enemy, so as to prevent them attempting to cross the river. We had already taken the precaution to remove all the boats from both sides of the river, in the vicinity of the Ghaut, so that they would be unable to cross over the guns without procuring fresh boats, or making rafts. Any demonstration, therefore, on the right (our) bank of the river would have prevented their doing this.

The officer in command, Major Thatcher, sent me back word that he was under strict orders to return to Meerut, after fulfilling his mission to beat back Walidad Khan's picquet; but that he would report the case to General Hewitt, who would probably make arrangements for stopping the passage. When General Hewitt received the report he ordered a Council of War, which decided upon not sending an opposing force, on the grounds that it would not be prudent to denude Meerut of troops at that juncture. I was, however, directed to send in reports every four hours, as to the movements of the enemy.

The day following I wrote to Thatcher thus—"Our Sowars (horsemen) have not yet returned from Ghurmuktesir, so we don't know what is going on. The Bareilly force may be within a few miles of us, for all we know. An hour or two will settle it one way or the other. The Goojurs, yesterday, after we left Malagurh, attacked the Jats at the village of Batounah, and there was a grand fight, many being killed and wounded on either side. The people, who report that the Mutineers are crossing the river, say that they have 10 to 15 elephants with them for the heavy guns, and that they are pulling down the choppers, *i.e.*, (the scantling of the roofs) of the houses, wherewith to make rafts. It may be all a lie, but it looks and sounds very fishy. If those fellows are marching on us in force, my best plan will be to let all the younger colts loose, and run the chance of their recovery when the row is over, and the mutineers have passed through to Delhi. Believe me, &c., C. D'Oyly."

I may mention here that the day before writing the letter just quoted, I had sent into Meerut some 400 to 500 of the older remounts to be stabled in the lines of the Cavalry stables of the 6th Dragoon Guards, of which regiment a portion had been sent off to join the besieging force at Delhi, and as regards the remainder of the young stock, I acted as suggested in my letter, and let them all loose when the mutineers were on the road to the Depot, and I may add that directly the rebel force had cleared off, I offered a reward of 10/- for every colt, and in this way recovered almost all of them.

Following out the orders received from the General at Meerut, I sent in messengers every four hours reporting the progress of the enemy. They were three or four days crossing the river, expecting every moment to be attacked by our troops. The reports ran thus—"The enemy are collecting boats from Rhamghat, and are making rafts." After four hours, I reported— "They are crossing their Infantry," and again—"They are crossing their guns." At this stage I received orders to retire into Meerut bringing the latest reports. It was then arranged that Captain Tyrwhitt, with his Irregular Cavalry, should precede me by some hours; that I being in charge of the Depot should wait until the last moment, and join him at Kurkoudah, a city half way on the road to Meerut, where he was going to halt for the night That morning, seeing that flight was inevitable and knowing that our houses would be plundered and probably burnt, I obtained a bullock cart, packed up my silver plate. a few articles and books I valued, and sent them to a native landowner, named Mohun Sing, a Jat, a good old fellow, who lived in a small fort, a few miles off, and asked him to take care of them until the rebellion was over, when I would reward him for his kindness. He willingly accepted the charge, and, I am sorry to add, it brought him into trouble, as I shall describe hereafter. I buried my wines in two large pits I had dug for the purpose in my garden, but all my household stores, such as hams, tongues, jams, sauces, pickles, and such like, I left in my store rooms, as also my furniture, including piano, pictures, &c., were left standing, being unable to procure carriage to remove them. These arrangements completed, and being left alone, with my horse ready saddled for a start, I waited till I should receive information of the approach of the enemy. The head of the column was soon descried in the distance by the dust it raised, and soon after we heard firing of muskets. I was surrounded by native messengers, who sorrowfully bid me adieu, kissed my feet, and were actually sobbing as I rode away. I turned my horse's head towards Meerut for my third and last flight.

On arriving at Kurkoudah I found our small camp pitched in the grounds attached to the Travellers' rest house. It was in a state of turmoil. Captain Tyrwhitt, the officer in command, had ordered commissariat supplies in the shape of grain, grass, &c., for his horses, and flour, milk, eggs, &c., for his men. Nothing had been got ready, so the Kotwal or Head Constable of the town was sent for, who pleaded in excuse, that he had done his best, but none were to be procured. The man was a Mahomedan, a rank rebel at heart. It was not a time to accept so frivolous an excuse, so he was threatened with condign punishment there and then, was kept as a hostage, while his messengers were hurried off for the supplies, which, I need hardly say, were very speedily forthcoming.

At dinner, that evening, it was arranged that I should go into Meerut, with part of the Cavalry as escort, to report the state of affairs to the General, leaving Captain Tyrwhitt to follow me some hours after with the remainder of the force, bringing the very last reports. Young Lyall, of the Civil Service, kindly offered to accompany me, and I gladly accepted his offer. We made an early start, about 3 a.m., and before starting I spoke a few words to the escort, forbidding anyone to leave the ranks on any pretext. This order was necessary, as in the stillness of the night we could distinctly hear the booming of the heavy siege guns at Delhi, and not a day passed without some of our soldiery deserting us to join their brother insurgents there. I was not aware, at the time, that part of the escort behind us belonged to a regiment, who had only a day or two previously mutinied and shot their officers at Mozuffernugur. The Adjutant of the regiment, a Lieutenant Smith, had been wounded, was being carried away in a dooley, or litter, when a native officer rode up and asked him if he was in pain. He replied that he was suffering much. The native officer pulled out his pistol from his holster, saying—"I will give you a pill to put you all right," and shot him. We had covered half the distance of our march, when, at early dawn, I spied one of the troopers stealing off in the distance. I halted the column and sent one of the escort to bring him back. I saw the men parleying together, and not liking the look of things, I turned to my companion, young Lyall, and asked him to gallop off and bring the two men back. He did so, and I was glad to see the men following him. On their joining the ranks, I addressed the delinquent, asking him if he had not heard the order that no man was to fall out without leave. He replied—"I was very thirsty, and I went off in search of water. I said—"You have disobeyed orders. Take off your sword. I shall march you in a prisoner." He was silent and did not stir. I repeated the order—"Take off your sword," no response, no movement. Again I ordered him to take off his sword, at the same time drawing my pistol from my holsterpipe. Seeing this, he slowly and sulkily unbuckled his belt, his sword was taken by my orderly, and he was a prisoner. I have always considered this a very critical moment. Any further delay in obeying my order and I must have shot him. There was no alternative, and then I expect it would have been a case of *sauve qui peut* for me and my young friend, for, no doubt, some of the men behind us were mutinous to the core, and once blood had been shed, there is no saying how the affair might have ended. It was a trying and an anxious moment, which happily terminated without bloodshed on either side. The rest of the escort, were, I think, taken by surprise, did not know what to do on the spur of the moment, and the hesitation saved us.

We completed our march into Meerut without further incident of interest. I immediately reported to the proper authorities the circumstances under which I had brought as a prisoner the mutinous trooper. He was tried by Court Martial, during the course of the day, and sentenced to be discharged. The only penalty inflicted on him was the loss of his horse (he was a Khuduspa, or owner of the horse he rode in the ranks) and his arrears of pay. He probably joined the insurgents at Delhi, the same night.

I may as well relate here the circumstances that occured at the Depot after our departure. The mutinous troops marched into the station with colours flying, and the bands playing "The British Grenadiers," and "Cheer boys, cheer." The General in command (Bakt Khan was, I think, his name) of the Artillery took up his head-quarters at Captain Parrott's house. It was in the centre of the Depot, while other officers occupied my house and the other bungalows. A Durbar was held in Bakt Khan's house, at which Walidad Khan, our old enemy, attended and doubtless all present believed, and not without reason, that the British power was at an end for ever. It had been threatening rain for some days. The Monsoon had not yet set in, but thunder clouds had been massing together, the lightening began to flash, and two days after the Brigade reached Haupper, the Monsoon began in earnest with a deluge of rain. It may be remembered that I mentioned previously having sent some of my private property to an old Jat, named Mohun Sing, who, I was told, buried it in his little fort. To the same refuge, an old Baboo, or native writer, attached to the Deputy Superintendent's

Office, betook himself. It was reported to the General in command that goods belonging to British officers, and also native clerks, were secreted in Mohun Sing's village. An order was consequently issued to the effect that a detail of Infantry, some Cavalry, and two field guns was to proceed to Mohun Sing's fort, and bring away the property and any Government servant who might be concealed there. They started with this object on the night on which the rainy season set in. As I said before, it was raining in torrents. The land lying between the Depot and the village was low and was soon inundated by the rivers, which surrounded the Depot, named the Chooeau and Kala Nudders. It became a perfect quagmire. The troops found great difficulty in moving. For the guns it became impossible. They sank up to the axles in soft mud, and the officer in charge, thinking it unwise to proceed without the guns, ordered the return of the force. Two or three days after this the Brigade proceeded on its way to Delhi, under orders from the King, and thus Mohun Sing escaped attack, the Baboo escaped capture, and my property escaped appropriation. The King also directed that none of the buildings, or the stables, hospital, granaries, stacks of hay and corn were to be destroyed, as he intended keeping all intact as a Cavalry Depot for his own Army. But the Officers' houses were completely gutted of everything. There was not even a nail left in the walls; the frames of the windows and doors were removed, and only the bare walls remained. All the property I had left had been plundered, with the exception of two cows and a pretty marble statuette, representing Cupid on Venus' shoulders. The statuette was called Cupid captured. These had been saved by an old native messenger of mine, named Nuttoo Sing, a resident of the neighbouring village, who after my departure and before the Sepoys arrived, had driven the cows away to his village and likewise taken away the Cupid. When he returned them to me, some months afterwards, he quaintly remarked that the marble child had met with an accident and had lost one of its arms. (He alluded to one of Cupid's wings, which had been broken off close to the shoulder) but that he thought I should not mind so much, as the baby had still three arms left, and he had never in his life seen a child with more than two. He had saved the statuette he told me, as, he thought, I valued it, and he was right there, for it was a marriage gift from a very dear friend. I gave him one of the cows as a gift, with which he was delighted, and thought himself well rewarded. I was touched with the old man's thoughtful consideration in the matter of the Cupid, although, probably, in regard to the cows, he may have thought that if there was to be an end to his master, he might as well be the possessor of the cows as the mutineers.

On the whole the native establishment worked well. Jumayut Sing, the head of the robbers, came to me soon after, and told me honestly all that he had done, and what had happened after I had left the Depot. He said that as the Brigade marched in, he went to meet them, gave them welcome, with fruit, milk, &c., and acted as conductor round the Depot. He was a clever, crafty old man, with a good deal of mother wit, and knew how to play his cards. I could not blame him for his expediency, in throwing in his lot with the mutineers. It was double dealing, doubtless, but his life and property were at stake, for he was a wealthy and leading man in the country, and it was taken for granted that if you did not side with the rebels, you were against them, and thus a difficult game was left to be played out.

Considering all things we escaped wonderfully well. Almost all the young stock were saved, the stallions were safe in the districts, the Depot buildings were left intact, with all the stores, so that when we returned to re-occupy the station, there was little to restore, so that, with the exception of the loss of some 20 or 30 Government bullocks, little harm was done.

CHAPTER III.

Creation and organisation of the Meerut Volunteer force—Am appointed Second in Command—Expedition against Seekree—Am wounded—Subsequent Expedition against Sah Mull and his Levies—His Defeat and Death—Night March and Return to Meerut—Attack on Galoutee—Sudden order to move to Thana Bawan, to relieve the Government servants besieged in that place—Arrive too late to rescue them—Their massacre—Return to Meerut—Disbandment of the Force—Receive letter of thanks from the Supreme Government.

———o———

At Meerut I found myself in comfortable quarters, sharing a house in the Artillery lines, with a Captain Salt and his wife. I had little to do, for to assist me in the care of some 450 remounts, I had a Captain, as assistant, a Veterinary Surgeon, and a large staff of non-commissioned officers. I therefore felt the want of active employment, and comparative idleness became irksome. Fortunately, at this juncture, the idea was conceived and speedily carried out to form a small force of volunteers, composed chiefly of cavalry, in view to enforcing the orders of the civil authorities, collect the revenue, over-rule the lawless, keep open the communication with Delhi, and guard the grand trunk road, north and south. I was offered the post of second in command of this little force, Colonel Williams and Captain Tyrwhitt being respectively commandant and adjutant. Better officers I could not have wished for, to get into shape the heterogeneous elements that composed the force. Although I had formerly been a Cavalry Adjutant, it was so many years since, that I had almost forgotten my drill book, so was forced to brush up my knowledge by attentive study of cavalry tactics. It was, however, congenial work to me and I entered with ardour on my new duties. We were at drill morning and evening, and the force being composed of intelligent men, indigo planters, tradesmen. and a good sprinkling of young cavalry and infantry officers, not yet posted to regiments, not to mention some civilians, who were invaluable owing to their local knowledge, it was not long before we got them into a fair state of discipline, and a knowledge of simple formations. They were all good horsemen, so we were spared the trouble of the riding school, and before many days an opportunity presented itself of trying their mettle. From a letter written to England, dated 23rd June, I make the following extract—" On Saturday I went out with a force to attack 2,000 of those wretched Goojurs, who had collected and were pludering our convoys on the road to Delhi. They, however, heard of our approach and made a bolt of it. We killed about 60, and burned five of their villages. I was in the saddle for nearly 12 hours on the 4th July. Thermometer in the house, 92 degrees. This is trying work, but we are healthy." In a letter, dated July 13th, I wrote thus—" As you have seen in the papers that I have been wounded, I write a few lines to set your minds at rest as to the extent of the wound, which I am thankful to say is trifling, although I had a very narrow escape."

The Volunteer Corps got orders to move out to attack the village of Seekree, in which it was reported that a force of these insurgent Goojurs had assembled, numbering about 2,000 men, after having plundered the neighbouring villages and murdered the inhabitants.

We accordingly marched at 2 o'clock at night, about 50 mounted volunteers, 30 infantry, and 2 mountain train guns. At daylight the rain commenced to pour heavily and continued all day, drenching us through and through. You know what the commencement of the Monsoon is in this country. We had it in all its violence on that day.

After a march of 15 miles we descried, in the distance, about 100 of the insurgents bolting across the country to the village, where the large body of them was assembled.

I took 10 file of Sikhs and galloped hard about two miles, getting to the other side of the village. Here we found them preparing to retreat, so placed videttes to check them until the remainder of the Cavalry should come up. Our guns came up shortly after, and fired shot and shell, but we could not turn them out of a walled enclosure, or small fort, where many had taken refuge and barricaded the large iron studded gates. About 15 of us dismounted and, after blowing in the gate, made a rush for the entrance. It was here I received a shot in the neck from a bullet, which had first struck the wall, was flattened by the blow, and then entered my neck, as flat as a shilling, and remained there until removed by Dr. Cannon, afterwards. In the meanwhile the flattened bullet remained in my neck while we rushed the gate. Here I got a severe sword cut on my hand, which divided the sinew to the bone. It was a nasty wound, but I was so excited that I did not feel it at the time, and was present until we had made good our entrance and killed 70 men in that enclosure. We then marched home. It was the most trying day's work I ever went through. From wet, exhaustion, want of food and loss of blood I fainted, a thing I never did before in my life. I was placed in a litter and reached cantonments about 6 p.m., got my hand and neck dressed, a cup of tea, took a strong opiate, and the next morning felt all right. I am now doing well and I hope to be in the saddle and at work again immediately. We have just heard of the fearful massacre at Jhansi. Penton Thompson, of the Artillery, has been wounded at Delhi, but he is doing well and the wound is not likely to be serious. Our posts from below are stopped, and we have not heard from Calcutta for six weeks

I give another extract from a letter, dated July 25th, 1857— "I have just returned from a weeks expedition into the district with a force from Meerut. We had a most trying march, crossed three rivers and had some hard fighting. We returned to Meerut after fulfilling our mission." Here it would be as well to give in greater detail an account of the expedition alluded to in the above extract, and I do not think I can do better than transcribe a portion of a work entitled the Khakee Ressalah, written by Wallace Dunlop, C.B., a civilian attached to our Volunteer Force, which was called the Khakee Ressalah, from the two Hindustani words—Khakee, dust colour, alluding to our uniform, and Ressala, a troop; in other words the dust coloured troop. He says—" Finding it absolutely essential that our enterprising enemy, Sah Mull, should be crushed, and a lesson inflicted on the rebel Goojurs. I had outlined a plan for attacking the southern villages by a rapid advance from Meerut of the Khakee Ressalah, and such help as the General would give us. It was certain that considerable danger attended the attempt, as forces would certainly be sent after us from Delhi, but I trusted to the rapidity of our movements, the increasing distance from Delhi as we advanced on Sah Mull's stronghold, and the prestige inseparable from audacity for success. Our worthy commandant of Volunteers objected to the plan as rash, but the commissioner supported my plan, and aided by a favouring fortune, we gained the greatest success ever won by our Volunteers."

In the latter end of July, two mountain guns, in the charge of two sergeants and eight native gunners, 50 mounted Volunteers, 40 H M. 60th Bifles, commanded by Captain Mortimer, marched from Meerut to the banks of the Hindua river. As our handful of men lay at Duchera, heavy firing commenced in the direction of Deolah, only seven miles distant. The distinct and rapid roll of heavy jezails and matchlocks, with the sullen booming of the guns at Delhi, little more than 20 miles distant, formed a fitting lullaby for those of us who were, next morning, to ford the Hindua and enter a territory from which we fully expected some of us would never return.

The reveille aroused us, after a brief rest, to ford the river, and as grey dawn broke, the cavalry went on at a gallop to surround Bussowd. A severe example was essential, and the slightest mawkish pusillanimity in such a case would have spread the flame of revolt throughout the district. All men, therefore, able to carry arms were shot down or put to the sword and their residences burnt. The only prisoners taken, some 15 in number, were ordered out of camp and executed in the evening, by order of the military commandant. It was a sad duty, just as we were sitting down to our mess dinner we heard two volleys of fire-arms, the death messengers of our 15 prisoners. Sah Mull now learnt that the sword alone could atone for his crimes; that he had roused a vengeance which could, when required, equal the sternest retribution he could inflict, women and children alone being exempted from destruction. I continue the narrative—The next morning, at two a.m., we marched to Barote. On reaching the town we were fired at from the walls. The enemy were about 3,000 strong They made three separate attacks, in large numbers, upon our small force, but we repulsed them, on each occasion, with great loss In leading a charge of cavalry upon a body of them we came upon Sah Mull himself, attended by his staff. He was killed by a young trooper in my squadron, who was himself wounded in the fight. We cut off his (Sah Mull's) head, placed it on a long lance, and marched with it through the villages, as a terror to other malefactors. This spear is now in my possession, and adorns my Hall.

After 14 hours in the saddle in a July sun, during which we had for some time been engaged with the enemy, with barely time for refreshment, we sat down to our mess dinner completely exhausted. We halted that night, but next day, at dinner, a paper was handed round, containing an order from the commandant, that immediately after dinner we were to resume our march. It was a heavy blow to us, who were looking forward to a sound sleep, after our fatigues of the preceding day, but the order must be obeyed. We learned that on the previous day, urgent requisitions for help from Delhi had been sent from the insurgents, with whom we had been engaged that day. To render assistance, two Infantry Regiments, 150 Cavalry, and four nine-pounder guns had been sent to attack us. Videttes and spies kept us well informed of the enemy's movements.

After dinner then, we began our march. The night was dark, and, just as we left Barote, rain began to fall heavily. We had two native guides to show us the way. In a few minutes I fell asleep on my horse. I was awaked by the order to halt. It appeared that the guides had lost their way. It was thought probable that they were in collusion with the enemy, and had intentionally misled us. They were at once placed under guard until daybreak, when if it was ascertained that they were guilty of treachery, they would then and there have been shot. In the meanwhile we were ordered to dismount, and in a few minutes we were on the ground holding our horses' bridles, and in another minute horses and men were fast asleep. It seemed but a moment after, that the trumpet sounded the reveille, but it was early dawn and the road we had missed was discovered to be some 200 yards to our left, so the poor guides' lives were saved. On arriving at the banks of the Hindua we descried, in the distance, the light scintellating on bayonets or swords, and after a few minutes, a body of troops appeared, whether friend or foe we knew not. We fell into fighting order, but were soon gladdened by the sight of a reinforcement, sent to us from Meerut, of a troop of carabineers and some artillery guns. Whilst halting on the banks of the stream I overheard an interesting conversation. Our Adjutant addressed a Native Officer of Cavalry and asked him if he was tired. He was a fine soldier-like looking man, with medals for service on his breast, and answered promptly—" Do I look like a man who would soon get tired ? " Captain Tyrwhitt said—" Certainly not, but we have undergone much fatigue, and it would not be surprising if you, as others of us, should feel the effects of it." He then continued—" How does it happen that you Rissaldar, sahib, still remain loyal to us and cling to our fortunes, when so many of your comrades have deserted us for the enemy." I may here remark that things were looking very black for us, at that moment. He replied—" My reason is this, I think in the end the British Government will win the day." It was an honest expression of opinion, for it will be observed that he made no mention of loyalty, or gave other grounds for his conduct, as gratitude or the honour of the flag. It was simply the question of self-interest that guided his conduct. And how can it be otherwise with the great mass of the Native Army (there are many notable exceptions) alien in race, religion and class feeling ?

After burning some disaffected villages we returned to our head-quarters at Meerut.

The next expedition on which we were sent I find described in a letter home, dated 9th August 1857—" Since I last wrote we have been employed on more service. A force of which our Volunteers composed part, marched from this all night with two Horse Artillery guns, Carabineers and Rifles."

The next day we heard the enemy, 2,000 strong, had taken up a position nine miles in our front, with five guns. We marched at two o'clock at night to attack them, came suddenly upon their advanced picquet. The 6th Dragoon Guards, who were leading, made a dash at them and charged through them cutting up a great number. We then brought up our guns and poured some rounds into them, when they broke and fled. We followed in skirmishing order, and came upon the position which the main body had taken up They had loopholed the walls and barricaded the entrance by felling trees, but we were too quick for them to make a defence 92 bodies were counted among the slain and numbers were wounded. The weather was very bad, the rain pouring heavily. Many of our men had no tents, but everything was borne cheerfully.

I find in my letter home the following, which I extract— "How many dear friends have gone in this fearful mutiny. Poor Edward D'Oyly, of the Artillery, killed in action at Agra. He was shot through the bowels by grape shot. He ordered his men to place him on the gun, and there he continued to fight his gun till the agony of inflammation rendered him helpless. He was then carried into Agra in a litter. The doctor gave him chloroform to allay his sufferings, but he died a few hours afterwards, as gallant, noble a fellow as ever breathed.

We have just received orders to march to-night to attack a Fort, 40 miles distant. We take eight guns, the Carabineers and Rifles, and expect to be absent about a week, and shall have some tough work.

You will be pleased to hear I have been thanked in Divisional Orders by name, and that the General is going to forward it, with some others, to the Commander-in-Chief."

Since writing the above the orders for our march have been countermanded, in consequence of a requisition from Delhi for the Rifles to take part, I suppose, in the assault on the city, which is expected to take place immediately. We were saved a very unpleasant march, for the night was most boisterous, blowing great guns and heavy rain.

I am astonished at the strength of my constitution in having stood the exposure to heat and rain so well as I have done. The excitement keeps me well I believe

As the assault on the city of Delhi was imminent, our force was ordered to take up a position near Haupper, to command the road from Delhi into Rohilcund, so as to cut off the fugitives from the city after it had been captured by our troops A spirited account of our proceedings is given in the following extract from a weekly paper—" Camp Haupper, dated 14th September, 1857. We have a pretty little force here, equivalent to at least three regiments of Sepoys, in the open. It consists of a troop of Carabineers, 60 Royal Rifles, the Volunteer horse, 300 Sikhs, 4 guns and 4 mortars. We could do—Oh! what could we not do, if they would only let us try? Well, we could take the Fort of Malagurh, and quaff champagne with our brother Volunteers there. There is no harm in giving you details of our force, as the Sepoys are equally well informed, and Walidad Khan has got the measure of every man in our camp. Every now and then he threatens a friendly village. We buckle on our armour and the truculent chief girds up his loins and runs! He is supported by the Jhansi Brigade, 400 Infantry, 400 Cavalry and 400 of his own cut and run levies—congenial spirits all."

On the 8th we marched against Pilkwa, the inhabitants numbered at 10,000. It was reported that they had been reinforced by a Sepoy Regiment. These villagers had refused to pay their revenue, but subsequently stated their willingness to do so, and requested that two messengers might be sent to receive it. The messengers were sent and instantly murdered. A patrol of 12 Carabineers and 12 Volunteer Horse proceeding towards the town, next morning, were fired at by matchlock men. A few of the men, armed to the teeth, were cut down by our troops, but being moonlight and the enemy in a dark jungle the patrol returned. Next morning we advanced to the attack, but, with a few exceptions, the enemy fled. We pursued them with our Volunteer horse, who cut down from 30 to 40. A few of the enemy showed great pluck and advanced sword in hand, calling us all sorts of opprobrious names. One man, while in the act of using his tongue rather freely, had his head completely severed from his body, with one swoop of a cavalry sabre. The lips still continued to move spasmodically in obedience to the last impulse and impression received from the brain.

The Rifles and Sikhs killed about 30 more, and there was plenty of plunder, which averaged about 10 rupees or £1 a head.

On the 10th there was an alarm in camp, and a report that Walidad Khan, with his Jhansi Brigade, and some thousands of Goojurs, were marching to attack us, and within six miles of our camp. The Carabineers, our Volunteer horse and two guns immediately were sent off at a canter to meet them, but the enemy had retreated to Galoutee, about 8 miles from Haupper.

We advanced to Galoutee to reconnoitre, and on reaching the town, were fired on from four nine-pounders. Our two six-pounders, under Tippy Smith, immediately replied. Our guns were admirably served, they found the range the first shot, and, after firing 14 rounds, completely silenced the enemy's battery. We gave them two more rounds for luck, and, as it now became dark, retired. We discovered next day that Cavalry, Infantry and Gunners had all bolted, abandoning their guns, so that, had we charged, we might have captured all their guns without the loss of a man. A charge would, however, have been very hazardous, the defeat of the enemy was so rapid and complete that we could not realise it, and imagined the retreat of the Cavalry to have been merely a feint. Their guns were flanked on the right by a village and a police station, and on the left by a wood and cultivation, so that their Infantry were invisible. The enemy lost 16 regulars killed and 35 wounded; among their dead were five artillerymen, killed by a shell; one gun dismounted and five horses left dead on the field. Our loss was trifling.

The discomfiture of Walidad Khan's regular force by 100 European Cavalry and two guns has opened the eyes of the Rajpoots, and they are now hurrying in with their revenue.

On the 21st of September our force was ordered to proceed to Thana Bowun, a beautiful city about 80 miles distant. The houses are built of stone, with large trees in the streets, and showing evidence of great wealth; several crumbling ruins attest its antiquity. We unfortunately arrived too late to save the Government servants and loyal subjects from massacre. The enemy had promised the Government servants their lives, on condition they gave up their arms. On complying with the demand, they were immediately attacked, and all, some 80 in number, treacherously murdered. They were Mahomedans. In vain they took refuge in a Mosque, and there in a sanctuary, plead for mercy from followers of a kindred faith. They were all barbarously murdered. I entered the Mosque. The sight was appalling. The walls were besmirched with blood; blood had spurted up on the ceilings, and the matting and floors were completely saturated. It was sickening to behold, and I hurried away from the horrible scene.

I was in command of all the Cavalry on this occasion. We had expected a vigorous resistance, but only overtook the rear guard of the fugitives. Our swords did their duty, and about 30 bearded sons of the prophet were sent to Paradise

Shortly after this we returned to Head Quarters at Meerut. And now the record of the Meerut Volunteer force is drawing to its close. After the successful assault of Delhi; the defeat of the King's troops; the shooting of the young Princes, the King's sons, by Captain Hodson, all now matters of history; the state of the districts rapidly improved. The might and majesty of British retributive justice had been made patent to all; lawlessness had been suppressed. Vengeance was satisfied. Mercy and conciliation followed, and there being no further call for our services, the force was disbanded, and the following letter was sent us in acknowledgment.

From the Official Secretary to Government of N. W. Provinces, to the Secretary of Government of India, Foreign Department, dated 12th February, 1858.—" Sir,—By direction of the Chief Commissioner I have the honour to submit for the consideration and orders of the Right Hon. the Governor General in Council correspondence marginally noted, elucidating the services performed by the Meerut Volunteer Horse, during the past disturbances. The Chief Commissioner concurs in opinion with the Commissioner of Meerut that Colonel Williams and Captains D'Oyly and Tyrwhitt, holding prominent parts in the Meerut Horse, have earned a title to some substantial recognition of the services rendered by them, services so undoubted that the Chief Commissioner has no hesitation in bringing the claims of these gentlemen to the favourable notice of the Supreme Government. Signed, C. B. Thornhill."

This letter was followed by one from the Supreme Government.

From G. F. Edmonstone, Esq., Secretary to the Government of India, dated 25th March, 1858. Home Department.—" Sir,—

I have the honour to acknowledge the receipt of Mr. Assistant Secretary Oldfield's letter, with enclosures, relating to the services performed by the Meerut Volunteer Force, during the late disturbances.

2.—In reply I am directed to state that the Governor General concurs in the opinion formed by the Chief Commissioner of the gallant and valuable service rendered by the Meerut Volunteers, and desires that his cordial thanks be conveyed to all those who thus assisted by their personal exertions and at the risk of their lives, in suppressing rebellion throughout the Meerut District and its vicinity, and in making the authority of Government felt and appreciated.

3.—His Lordship's thanks are more especially due to the civilians in the force, who, when their own functions were in abeyance, did not fail to undertake military duty in support of the Government they served, and to Major Williams and Captains D'Oyly and Tyrwhitt, to whose professional knowledge and direction and praiseworthy zeal, the organisation of the Corps and its efficiency may be assumed to be mainly due.

4.—The Governor General will recommend the Honourable Court of Directors to grant steps of brevet rank to the above named officers for their undoubtedly valuable services. I have, &c., G. T. Edmondstone, Secretary to the Government of India."

Thus acknowledged, the brief but brilliant career of the Meerut Volunteers closed. Its members returned to other duties and, varied by the use of the pen, have proved themselves equally able and willing with the sword. They have doubtless in after years reflected with pleasing retrospect, on adventures and endurances by flood and field, scorching suns, drenching rains, forced marches, bivouacs by the camp-fire, enlivened at times by song and jest, which served for the moment to cheer the saddened heart, rouse the dejected, and threw a slight gleam of sunshine on our perilous and depressing life. But we acted throughout by a sense of what we owed to our country, and every man in the force did his very best to do his duty.

CHAPTER IV.

Leave to the Hills—Visit Delhi—Join force to convey guns and stores to the Advancing Column—Attached to the 6th Dragoon Guards—Cavalry action at Gungeree—Action at Pultiali—A Ressaldar blown away from a gun—March to Mynpoorie and action—Captain Hodson, his character and acts—Arrival at Cawnpore, the entrenchments and well—To Allahabad by road and rail, take charge of an Insane—Arrival at Ghuzeepore—General Remarks.

———o———

At this time I received promotion in the Department and was ordered down country to take up the duties vacated by Colonel Apperley, who had been sent to the Cape of Good Hope to purchase remounts for the Army. But the roads were not safe and I was forced to wait a favourable opportunity to join any troops that might be proceeding in that direction. As I could hear of no suitable escort at the time I went up to the hills for a few days change of air and scene

In a letter written at this time I find the following— " October 13th, 1857. The course of the last five months is like a dream to me, now that I am at rest and have a few quiet moments to myself after the stirring scenes we have lately witnessed. I can hardly yet realise that my lot in life is so completely changed; that a few short months have rendered many miserable and wretched, who, at the beginning of the year were full of hope and life. Poor Greathed is gone—he died of cholera. I cannot help thinking of the happy days we spent in his house, where we met so many friends, now no more. It is very sad to see the number of widows up here, the number of wounded officers and soldiers, and of children in mourning for their parents. What a blow has been struck us in the confidence of power and authority. The hatred that has been shown to all Christians and the cruelty that has accompanied it, is not to be explained. You have probably long ago heard of the sad fate of the poor Sowisses at Futteygurh. I have never alluded to it. The subject is too sickening and too heart rending to dwell upon."

On my return to Meerut on the 22nd November, I wrote the following letter to England—" Meerut, Nov. 22nd. This morning I received your letter, dated 8th October, in which you mention having heard of my death, through the Adjutant General's Office in Calcutta. I cannot think how the report originated,* for considering the exposure I have undergone since the 10th of May, my health has been remarkably good, and I am very well now, thank God, barring a severe cold that I caught in the Palace at Delhi, by sleeping in a room that had just been whitewashed and the walls of which were not dry. In my last letter I told you of my return to Meerut and the orders I had received to proceed down country on the first favourable opportunity to take charge of the Deputy Superintendent's Office in the Central Studs, vacant by the appointment of Colonel Apperley to buy horses at the Cape of Good Hope, for the Cavalry and Artillery. As a column was expected to start from Delhi shortly, in order to convoy stores and carriage down to Havelock's force at Cawnpore, I took the opportunity to accept the offer of a friend of mine, Major Tombs of the Horse Artillery, to take a seat in his dog cart to drive over to Delhi to see the place, and meet my friend, Sir Edward Campbell of the 60th Royal Rifles, an old brother A.D.C. on the Marquis of Dalhousie's staff. I cannot adequately describe the interest I took in the visit. I went all over the ground held by our troops during the four months' siege. I saw every spot, where a shell had burst into a picquet, or a rocket had taken off a man's leg I went into our breeching batteries, and into the trenches where our brave fellows poured up on the day of the assault. I saw the houses riddled with round shot, grape, and musket balls, where the enemy had held positions in the city, fighting obstinately. I saw the doorsteps where poor Captain Douglas, commanding the Palace Guard, was shot down by the troopers of the 3rd Cavalry, when he went down to speak to them at the doors. I saw the walls and floors stained black with blood, where those

---

*A telegram was sent home stating that Captain C. D'Oyly had been killed in action. It was a mistake for Captain E. D'Oyly, of the Artillery, who was killed at Agra.

poor girls, Miss Jennings and Miss Clifford, were foully and cruelly murdered, by being hacked to death with swords by those cowardly ruffians, as they were eating their breakfast in one of the rooms of the King's Palace. It is a sight never to be forgotten, and the like of which I never wish to see again. The case of poor Miss Jennings was particularly sad. She was the daughter of a clergyman, and was engaged to be married to a Lieut. Thomason of the Engineers, a son of the Lieutenant Governor of the N. W. Provinces. She was a beautiful girl, good, honest and English, and it is said was spending the day with Captain Douglas in the Palace. They were at breakfast when the servant said that some Sepoys wished to speak to him. He went down suspecting nothing, was met at the foot of the stairs by the mutineers, who riddled him with bullets. They then went up stairs. The servant was handing a glass of water to Miss Jennings, when a bullet shivered the glass to pieces, and the soldiers then rushed in and cut up the whole party with their swords. I can hardly believe in such cruelty, but there was the evidence of the blood dashed about the walls and partly down the stairs, where these poor girls sunk down from loss of blood. But why dwell upon this dreadful tragedy ? I will turn to happier topics. I have just returned from a few days visit to Haupper, to inspect my farm there. The hay crop is being carted and stacked, a magnificent crop, and everything looks so peaceful and quiet, that one can hardly believe that all over the country, battles are going on and lives lost by hundreds. When I was there I heard of the victory of our troops over the Joudpore Legion, near Delhi. The enemy, said to be 8,000 strong, were beaten with great loss and six of their guns taken. Colonel Gerard, commanding our force, was killed. When I was at Delhi I went with Sir Edward Campbell, who is one of the prize agents, to see the plunder of the city taken after the assault, and which was sold at public auction, the proceeds to be distributed among the troops. There were some beautiful jewels, gold embroidery, saddle-cloths, covered with pearls and other precious stones, and every description of jewellery. I saw some long maces, which I was told had been held by servants surrounding the King, and bought one, for which I gave two gold mohurs, or 32s. in our money. When I took it home and had it cleaned I found it was silver, and thinking I had made a good bargain, I wrote to the prize agent to say that I would take another at the same price. Unfortunately, in the meanwhile, they had discovered that I had got mine too cheap, and wrote me word that I had (unintentionally of course) made too good a bargain, but that if I would send them 60 rupees (*i.e.*, £6 in our money) I might have one*. I sent them the money. I have also got some arms, which I took in our various expeditions, which I will also send you. Also a book which I took out of a beautiful Jain temple. There were numbers of them lying about, but no one took the trouble to pick them up. The book is one of the Hindoo shasters, or holy records. To-day I hear that a column is likely to start on the 2nd December, and that we are likely to meet with some opposition, from various bodies of the enemy's troops, I trust we may give a good account of them."

A few days after my return from Haupper, I learned that a considerable force, under Brigadier General Seton†, was to move down country in charge of a convoy, as I mentioned above. I joined the force and immediately placed my services at the command of the General in command. I was at first ordered to do duty with Hodson's horse. Captain Hodson was at the head of the Intelligence Department, a fine, bold, dashing soldier, who had been authorised to raise a body of horse for immediate service. It was this corps I was ordered to join, but finding that my old friend, Captain George Wardlaw, was with the force with a squadron of his Regiment, the 6th Dragoon Guards, the Carabineers, I asked leave to be allowed to serve under him, in preference to Captain Hodson, whose newly raised Regiment was only half drilled and disciplined. I was allowed to join the Carabineers, and was with them for the rest of the march, as shall be described.

*I have the pair of chobas now decorating my Hall.
†Afterwards Sir Thomas Seton, K.C.B.

The actual marching was very tedious, for we had a large convoy to protect, with some heavy guns, drawn by bullocks, and I think we barely traversed two miles an hour. The distance of each march was some 10 to 12 miles, so that we took five or six hours to accomplish it. When we passed through Haupper, I found poor old Mohun Sing, the Jat to whom I had entrusted my property and who had buried it, as I have mentioned before, and nearly lost his life for doing so, standing waiting for me, jubilant and happy, with the bullock cart and my large camel trunks covered with earth and not a thing missing. I gave him a good present, and likewise a testimonial of his conduct to submit to the Government when the rebellion was over, and a strong recommendation that he should be well rewarded. I am glad to state, that my letter was successful in getting him some villages, when the rewards for loyalty by our Government were distributed.

I will here give an extract from a letter I wrote to my father describing our march—"Camp, 60 miles from Allyghur and 40 from Futteyghur. When I last wrote to you I was on the point of starting with a column of troops, conveying stores and carriage to assist the Commander-in-Chief to move up country. I anticipated having a brush with the enemy and my expectations have been realised. On reaching Allyghur we left the whole of the carriage in the fort and moved on with the fighting portion to meet a body of the enemy that was marching from Futteygurh to attack us. We were here joined by two guns, nine-pounders, and a wing of the 3rd European Infantry, from Agra. Our force, previous to the junction of the Agra troops, consisted of a squadron of Carabineers, a detail of the 9th Lancers, under Captain Head, the remnant of the 1st European Fusileers, Turner's troop of Horse Artillery, to which Penton Thompson is attached, two 16-pounders, one 24-pounder Howitzer, and a 5-inch mortar, Hodson's horse, numbering 600, and Stafford's 7th Sikh Infantry. Total about 1,800 to 2,000 of all arms. The enemy was reported to be about 26 miles to the eastward. We covered the distance in two marches and we then heard that the enemy were still in our front. We marched on the third day to a place called Gungeree, about seven miles from Khasgunge, which you will find in the map. We had just had a late breakfast and I had retired to my tent, taken off my sword and coat, and was lying down to try and get a little sleep, when I heard the Infantry bugles sounding the alarm, and the Cavalry trumpets sounding boot and saddle. I instantly jumped up, buckled on my sword and rushed out to see what was up. An officer, who had been sent out to reconnoitre, came galloping back to say that the enemy were advancing on our camp in four columns. I mounted my horse and rode off to join the 6th Dragoon Guards. The officers attached to the squadron at the time were Captain George Wardlaw, in command, Captain Hudson, Lieutenant Baker Russell, Cornet Vyse, and Captains D'Oyly and Sandford, of the Bengal Cavalry doing duty. We formed on the extreme right, and the enemy's fire from one nine-pounder and two sixes began to open upon us with shot and shell. Luckily they fell short. Our Artillery, under Colonel Bishop, had already moved forward. Mr. Cracroft Wilson, who was attached to the force as a political officer, rode up and said the Brigadier-General wished us to move on in support of the Artillery. We were glad to do so, as the enemy had begun to find our range and the round shot were bobbing over our heads in a very unpleasant manner. Captain Light, of the Artillery, who was acting on that day as galloper to the Brigadier-General, came galloping up and ordered us to charge, he accompanying us. As we neared the enemy, our pace increased. They had found our exact range and their round shot came bowling into us, making havoc in our ranks. We then faced three discharges of grape shot, which emptied many saddles. With a cheer we dashed into their guns, and then at their cavalry and infantry in support. The enemy broke, the day was ours, with their guns in possession. Poor George Wardlaw was shot through the head, close to the guns. Cornet Vyse had been shot alongside of me, with three bullets through him, one through his mouth and two through his body. He was a brave, gallant young fellow and had only left Eton a few months before. I myself had a most narrow escape, the end of my pistol was carried away by a shot, which would, probably, have entered my body, had it not been deflected by the butt of the pistol. Just as we neared the guns, some irregular cavalry charged us. One made for me and brought his sword down on my head, but my helmet saved me. At the same time I gave him point, and ran him through, and rolled him head over heels. A Dragoon behind me called out—"The beggar's all right, sir!" meaning that he was done for. After capturing the guns a halt was called to collect stragglers and the wounded. We had lost out of 85 men, who had commenced the charge, 24 killed and wounded. Captain Head, of the Lancers, was hit by a shot, which broke his arm and then entered his body. I shall mention him again farther on. On Captain Wardlaw's death, the command of the squadron fell to Captain Hudson, who ordered the men to dismount and skirmish with their carbines, through the fields, covered with wheat and urrah crops. Before the charge Captain Sandford had been ordered with a division to skirmish to our right, and Lieut. Baker Russell with a similar party to our left. On Captain Hudson taking command, he requested me to go in search of Baker Russell and order him to join the squadron. I did so, but it was not a pleasant duty by any means, as some of the enemy were lying concealed in the crops, and fired at me as I galloped past. I accomplished my errand, however, without being touched, and on returning with Baker Russell and his men, we heard some shots fired, and I saw a small party of troopers collected together. I rode up and saw Captain Hudson on the ground I jumped off my horse, ran up and found him dying. There was froth on his lips. He gave one deep sigh and expired. I put my hand on his heart, but life was extinct. We placed his body on a gun wagon and carried him back into camp, with the other dead bodies and the wounded. On arriving in camp, I met the Brigadier-General, Sir Thomas Seaton, who said—"Captain D'Oyly, I heard that Captain Head of the Lancers has been very hard hit. Go to Dr. Brougham, enquire the nature of the wound and bring me word." I left and a few minutes afterwards met Dr. Brougham, who said—"He is as bad as can be ; I would amputate his arm, but he will probably die of the shot in his body during the night, so why torment him with an operation ? " The doctor was not right in his judgment, for the wounded arm recovered and the shot in his side, though it nearly killed him at the time, became embedded, and he was afterwards sent home with invalids to England, where he one day fell down dead suddenly, playing billiards in Dublin. This is the story we heard. On that evening I found him sitting on an easy couch, drinking champagne, as white as a sheet. I wished him good night, thinking I should never see him alive again. On reaching my tent I found an order waiting for me, directing me to take charge of the funeral party, to bury the officers and men killed in the action. We buried them that evening, the bodies wrapped in their blankets. We were lighted by torches held aloft. It was a solemn scene : in the middle of a wild plain, the Dragoons carrying the litters, in the distance, the lights of our large camp, and some of our brave soldiers sobbing as we lowered the bodies into their last home, and then the burst of the three volleys of musketry, which concluded the service, and we all retired to our tents, thinking whose turn it might be next, for we expected to meet the enemy again on the morrow. In the morning, these men full of life and hope, in the evening, laid out in their beds looking happy, though dead ; for it is a remarkable fact that men killed by a bullet, have a very different appearance to those killed by the bayonet All the officers were great favourites, particularly poor George Wardlaw, who was beloved by his men, a finer, braver, more gallant soldier never lived. I liked him very much, and had seen a good deal of him lately, as we had been fellow campaigners during the last three months. He was at Sherborne School, knew Dorsetshire well, and was a friend of Sir Edward Baker's of Ranston. If you see Sir E. Baker you may tell him that his loss is deeply felt by all ; that he had the reputation of being one of the best cavalry officers with the Army ; and that he died a gallant death after leading as glorious a charge as was ever made."

We marched the next day to Khasgunge, finding many dead bodies on the road, who had been wounded by our grape. We marched again this morning, and, on the road, were told that the enemy, with seven guns, was waiting for us; but as we approached, we ascertained that they had retired during the night. We came upon their rear-guard who were all cut up. They have fallen back, it is said, upon some re-inforcements posted at a place called Puttiali. We march there to-morrow and hope they will give us the chance of a fight.

December 18th, 1857. The day previous a capture had been made by some men of Hodson's horse. A Ressaldar,* a pensioner of the Government for 30 years' service, had concealed himself in a house after the battle of Gungeree, already described. He was caught jumping from a back window into a garden; was brought before the Brigadier-General, who ordered him to be immediately tried by Court Martial. After trial he was sentenced to be blown away from a gun in the presence of the troops. It appeared, from the evidence against him, that before the commencement of the Mutiny, he had made a pilgrimage to Mecca, for he was a Mahomedan, had there visited the shrine of the prophet, and had consequently gained the odour of sanctity and had become a double-distilled Mussalman, and more bitterly hostile against the opponents of his religious faith. He had two sons in the Native Army, both officers of rank. On his return to Bombay he found the whole country in a blaze with the mutiny of the Army. Notwithstanding he had eaten the Government salt, as the native term expresses devoted service, and was in the receipt of a handsome pension, he at once joined the ranks of the rebels, and his first appearance on the scene was in the action narrated above. He certainly deserved his fate if ever man did.

That morning we received confidential orders to be ready in case an attempt should be made at rescue. A body of Mooltanee

* A Native Captain of Cavalry.

Horse had just joined us, in great part Mahomedans, and therefore sympathising with the prisoner. The European and Sikh portion of the troops were likewise warned to be ready to fire a volley into the native troops, if they attempted a rescue, and we were to charge them when they broke. All this was arranged on the quiet, and at three o'clock, p.m., the execution parade was ordered. We formed up into two sides of a square, and the doubtful native troops formed the third side; the fourth side left open. A six-pounder gun, manned by European Artillery, was run into the centre, immediately in front of the place we were posted in. The Brigadier-General and his staff appeared on the scene and the prisoner was ordered to be brought forward to hear the sentence of the Court Martial, which contained his death warrant. He was placed about 40 yards in front of the gun, which was to blow him to atoms. He showed no signs of fear, but stood with arms crossed, his head thrown back and in a somewhat defiant attitude. He was dressed in the full dress uniform of his corps, red jerkin, with gold lace and medals on his breast. Captain Osborne, the interpreter, was directed to read out the proceedings of the Court Martial and sentence. When the latter was read, the prisoner showed by a slight movement of his features that he felt his last moments had arrived. The port-fire of the gun was then suddenly lighted. The prisoner was marched forward towards the gun. His demeanour was somewhat theatrical, but grand withal, and one could not help feeling admiration and sorrow for the misguided man, as he marched so bravely to his death. In a loud voice he quoted verses from the Koran, but the Sikhs behind him, bitterly hostile to his religion and unwilling to allow a dramatic display, gave him sundry pushes from behind, which considerably disconcerted him and spoiled the effect. On reaching the gun he stood proudly before it, expecting in that position, every moment to be blown away, but two European gunners ran out, pinioned his arms and in a minute, fastened him to the muzzle; the port-fire was applied to the priming, and in an instant his soul was launched into eternity. His body was blown into a thousand fragments, but his head and feet flew backwards, and a piece of his ribs fell upon my saddle. The Mahomedan troops never moved, calculating, probably, that the gun that had just put an end to their co-religionist, could and would be turned upon them, if they showed the slightest disposition to attempt a rescue. So ended an interesting, but terrible scene.

December 18th, 1857. "I wrote to you two days ago giving you an account of our action on the 14th, in which we made a glorious charge and captured three guns, but with such a serious loss. I then said I hoped we should meet the enemy again the following day. We did so. We had marched about nine miles when firing was heard in our front. Our advanced picquet had come within range of the enemy's guns. I was with the Carabineers as before. We galloped up and took post on the right of the line, Hodson's horse being to our right.

Our Artillery was pushed on, and opened fire. A brisk cannonading took place. We had got within the range of their fire, and shot from a nine-pounder came bowling over us. We were ordered to move out of the range of their shot. Our Infantry and heavy guns advanced in the centre, our Horse Artillery guns on the right and left. We got within grape distance and the enemy then commenced to retire. Their Cavalry had bolted long before. We were then ordered to the front in pursuit. On we went at the gallop, cutting up fellows right and left, and for six miles we kept it up in the direction of Futteyghur. All their guns, 14 in number, camp equipage, ammunition, and baggage fell into our hands We followed the enemy as far as the banks of Boodh Gunga, the old stream of the Ganges, when our trumpets sounded the halt. The stream at which we arrived, presented, at that spot, a large pond or lake, into which many of the enemy had thrown themselves, to escape by swimming to the other side. The Carabineers unslung their carbines, and began popping at their heads as they appeared above the water; some, but very few, escaped; one after another they were struck by bullets and sunk; soon all was over, and as the enemy had entirely dispersed and not one seen on the horizon, we rejoined the column and returned to camp."

The same evening I bathed and dressed, and on looking out through the cane blinds of my tent, I observed a guard with a prisoner. I had my revolver with me. We always wore them in those days in our belts, and I followed the party to ascertain what they were about. I was told that the prisoner in their charge was a young soldier, who had been taken with arms in his hands, fighting against us, had been tried by Drum-head Court Martial and ordered to be shot outside the camp. At this time we had arrived at the spot fixed for the execution. There were eight rank and file forming the firing party. The prisoner was a fine young soldier, about 21 years of age, belonging to the 56th Regiment Native Infantry. His eyes were bandaged, he was placed against a tree, and the firing party, at the command of the officer, fired a volley. It is usual on such occasions to have only one half of the muskets loaded with ball cartridge, the other half with blank cartridge This arrangement is made with the laudable intention to soften, as far as possible, the terrible feeling that one's own arm and firelock has been instrumental in taking away the life of a fellow creature, and may be a comrade. No member of the firing party is told whether his firelock is loaded with ball or not. They are directed to fire straight at the heart. Whether intentionally or through nervousness, only one bullet, from the whole firing party, struck the prisoner and that on the leg. He was knocked over and writhed in agony. The officer in command, seeing me standing by armed, asked me to put an end to his suffering, which I did at once by shooting him through the head, thus saving him further pain. But the act of doing so, gave me a shock which I took some days to get over. It is a very different matter to take life in the heat of action, to shooting a man in cool blood, as on the occasion described.

I find the following in my next letter to England. Speaking of the action at Puttiali, I wrote—"The enemy had been reinforced the day before our arrival by troops and guns from Futteyghur. They only stood to their guns for about an hour, when their chief set the example of flight. A few men fought well at the guns. My charger is knocked up and lame by yesterday's gallop, and I have no other, so I shall have to trudge the rest of the march on foot. However, I am well and pretty strong. None of our Artillerymen were touched, except one man, who has lost some fingers."

December 20th. "We have just heard that the C.I.C., Sir Colin Campbell, has had an action with the Gwalior contingent and given them a good dressing, taking 38 guns, with ammunition, stores, &c. We also hear of the death of General Havelock, but whether by disease or killed in action is not stated.

We moved our camp yesterday, on hearing that a force sent by Khan Bahadur Khan, of Bareilly, had crossed over the river yesterday morning, with the purpose of attacking us. They are said to have guns. They had not heard of our action of the 17th, but on learning it, they retired immediately.

Greathed of the Engineers is with our column. We had a long talk of Dorsetshire and Dorset people yesterday. Poor Mrs. Greathed, widow of Harvey Greathed, is at Mynpoorie, with her sister, Mrs. Trench. They say she has aged very much since her affliction.

The Chief we hear is marching on Futteyghur, so it will fall to his force to disperse the enemy here. I had hoped that our column might have been allowed to do it, but we are on our return now to continue our escort to the convoy. Poor Captain Head, of the 9th Lancers, who was shot down by grape at Gunzeree, is doing wonderfully well, his arm it is thought may be saved. The only fear is on account of the bullet in his body, as the doctors cannot ascertain which direction it has taken, and fear that, in working itself out, it may come in contact with some of the vital parts, as the lungs, liver or heart. I am very much interested in the poor fellow, he is so patient and gentle and is such a proper, good feeling man, Irish and very good looking."

December 18th, 1857. " Since I last wrote we have been making double marches in order to attack the Mynpoorie Rajah, Tej Singh, who with about 3,000 men and guns has taken up a position to oppose us.

The day before yesterday, while on the march, we met a miserable looking object in the shape of a native, who was travelling along the road. He looked as if he had not a penny in the world, and his dress consisted of a few rags. He, however, stopped our advance guard and enquired who was in command of the column, as he had a message to deliver. He was sent back and confronted with Sir Thomas Seaton, the General in command, and being asked his business, he took his stick, a bamboo cane, and opened it. It was hollow, and had been most beautifully and accurately fitted to hold a piece of paper. so closely rolled up that you might have put it into a very small thimble. The paper was unrolled and found to contain most valuable information. It had been sent by some well wisher of the Government to give us warning that the enemy had erected a strong battery of guns to command the road by which we were to advance on the position. It further stated that the man had been promised 100 rupees if he delivered the note safely. It was money well spent. Had we not been cautioned, and had we marched direct upon the battery, we should have certainly lost many lives. As it was we made a flank movement with our Cavalry and Artillery, took them almost in reverse, and with our guns pounded them in flank. This alteration in our tactics completely puzzled them and after firing about a dozen rounds at us, which did little harm, they made a clean bolt of it, leaving their guns, ammunition and equipage in our hands. We then marched straight for the Rajah's Palace. He had taken flight early in the morning, and was, therefore, not found at home. Since leaving Meerut on the 7th inst., we have taken 25 guns, with ammunition wagons, stores and camp equipage.

We are now encamped on the parade ground, at Mynpoorie. Close to us is the Station Church, a very pretty little building. These wretched rebels have destroyed all they could inside, defacing and throwing down the monuments in the churchyard. All the houses of the residents have been burned down and plundered. In the city, yesterday, were found many dresses. with other articles of female attire, besides children's frocks. &c.

Some prisoners were taken; tried by Court Martial and sentenced to be hung. Amongst them was an old Jemadar,* who had been 40 years in the service! a grey headed old veteran. As the party of prisoners were being escorted by a guard taking them to execution, a sergeant of the 1st European Fusileers, now the 101st Fusileers, appeared holding a Sepoy by the arm. He was an Irishman, who having saluted the officer in charge said— 'If you plaze, sorh, I have just found an armed Saypoy in a hut.' The Officer, without further parley, ordered him to be tacked on to the rear of the other prisoners, and in five minutes he was hanging from a bough of a tree, with 15 other prisoners. It appeared that the sergeant being very tired after the march and action of the morning, found his way into a native hut, took off his accoutrements and lay down to sleep. After a doze he rose and looking about him thought he saw some movement in the corner of the hut. He approached the spot, and, raising some straw, dragged forth a Sepoy from his hiding place, who had also fallen asleep, after covering himself with straw for concealment. The sergeant seized him and brought him out just as the procession of doomed prisoners was passing by. It was a regular case of 'long rope and short thrift' for the unlucky soldier."

After the capture of Mynpoorie, we continued our way down the grand trunk road, with the convoy. It was at this time

* Native Officer of Infantry.

that Captain Hodson, chief of our Intelligence Department and commandant of Hodson's horse, left our camp on horseback, with some two or three men of his own regiment as escort, to ride some 80 miles to attempt to open up communication with the column that was marching up the country. I must digress here to say a few words in regard to this remarkable man, celebrated for his inestimable services during the seige of Delhi, his capture of the Princes, the King's sons; his shooting them down in the public thoroughfare of the Imperial city, as a terror and warning to all rebels against the British Government. The name of Hodson resounded throughout the whole of the civilised world, and, doubtless, you might search the kingdom through and fail to find one so admirably qualified, by character and professional attainments, for the rôle he was called on to fill during those troublous times. A fine horseman, a skilful swordsman, with good constitution, undeniable courage, full of action and resource; he was one in a thousand, aye, in ten thousand! His faults and failings I will not discuss here. They have been canvassed and condemned by far abler pens than mine, and I here only wish to add my tribute as a soldier to his exceptional qualifications as a leader of men, and, I will further add my belief, that our success at Delhi was, in great measure, due to the untiring zeal, energy and military knowledge he displayed in so remarkable a manner. His ride, alluded to above, is full of incident, but I must not enlarge further on that theme, which forms a separate history. I will simply add that after running serious risk of capture and death, he effected his purpose in safety, and was afterwards killed at the storming of Lucknow, a loss to the army almost irreparable.

We continued our march, and at Bewar we formed a junction with another column of troops, under the command of the Hon. Colonel Walpole, two regiments of the Rifle Brigade, Artillery and other details.

Here with great regret I bid adieu to the column. I had formed friendships, which are rapidly cemented in the hours of peril. It is in such times one soon discovers a man's true character, the wheat is severed from the chaff, and many a man displays real grit, which in the times of peace lies hidden and unrecognised.

I joined Greathed, of the Engineers, in a dog cart to Cawnpore, where I went to the fort and put up with an old pal of mine, Albert Austen, of the Horse Artillery, and the next day sallied forth with him to view the entrenchments where Sir Hugh Wheeler and his gallant force held out so heroically against the mutinous troops· It seemed to me marvellous, that a garrison could have held its own, so long as it did, against such an overpowering force of Artillery. We went to the Ghaut, where I was shown the place from which the masked battery opened and poured death and destruction upon our poor defenceless troops, deprived of arms, and encumbered, as they were, with the women and children. It was too sad to dwell long there, so we then went to the house where so many of our countrymen and women were so foully murdered, and to the well into which they were thrown. A beautiful garden now adorns the sacred spot, and the famous statue, by Marochetti, stands in the centre of an ornamental enclosure, as a lasting memorial to the martyrs who died there.

I left Cawnpore by carriage and joined the railway half way between that station and Allahabad. Dr. Macaulay was my travelling companion. At the railway station a carriage drove up, with a sergeant of the Army Service Corps on the box, and inside was a traveller with his head shaved, just arrived from Lucknow. He proved to be a Dr. A , an insane. On taking our seats, (there were only two first class carriages) we found, one of them had been engaged by some merchants from Meerut. Just before we started the sergeant came up to our carriage in great distress, and said he could not persuade his charge to take his seat. I said—"If you cannot manage him, is it likely that I can do so " He replied—" He might pay more attention to an officer and obey your orders, for he certainly won't obey me." I got out and went to the doctor, and said—"Come along, you'll be too late, if you don't get into the carriage at once. The starting bell has rung." He then said—"I am not going by the train." I said—"Nonsense, how do you propose to go?" "I am going, he said, to hire a pony and ride all the way." I said—"You can't get a pony here," and I took him gently by the collar of his coat to lead him to the train. To my surprise he said—"If you won't hold me, I will come." He then followed me quietly, to the evident satisfaction of the sergeant and the station-master, anxious to start the train. He attempted to jump out of the carriage at Khagah, where we stopped for a few minutes to give water to the engine, but we restrained him, and on arrival at Allahabad, made him over safely to an European Guard, who had been sent by the Brigade Major to receive him.

I left Allahabad two days after, by carriage, for Benares, and arrived at my destination, Ghazeepore, without further incident. I make the following extract from a letter, dated 19th January, 1858—"I have arrived at the first Depot in my jurisdiction, after a long and tiresome six weeks' journey from Meerut, having been present at three actions and the capture of 25 guns. I came on with the convoy as far as it went on its way to Cawnpore; thence by transit carrriage, 66 miles, and rail, 56 miles, to Allahabad; thence to Benares by carriage, and so on here. You cannot understand the feeling of rest and security and of being in a comfortable furnished house once more, after the turmoil and exposure and work of the last eight months. I am staying with the Depot Officer, a Captain Jackson, whose house is on the banks of the river, which flows along so quietly below us; no sound to disturb the air, beyond the occasional dip of the oars of some heavy country boat, dropping lazily down the stream. I can hardly realise the fact, that up country war is still raging; that a few weeks ago saw me charging a battery of guns, with the cheers and death groans of many a gallant fellow ringing in our ears. Here appears no sign of strife, the country is quiet all round, cultivation goes on as usual. The native farmers have all their mares and young stock, and no loss has been sustained by the Government.

Occasionally a large steamer goes fizzing by, with its big paddle wheels, lashing quiet Gunga* into a sea. The change is to me so great! and the comfort complete."

Here ends the narrative of my personal experience of eight months of the mutiny year, 1857. I pause to ask—Is there no useful lesson to be learned? No moral to be drawn from the foregoing simple recital of events? I think so. Statesmen, responsible for the integrity of the British possessions in the East; for the safety and security of the life and property of the teeming millions subject to our sway have learned a dearly bought lesson; that it is not safe to place entire and implicit trust (without the necessary safeguards) in an alien army, drawn from a distinct race, differing in religious faith, bound by no tie, but that of self interest, and subject to sudden panics and incontrollable impulse, when actuated by fear that their religion is the object of assault. The weak points in our armour were revealed and mended; the evils inherent in our former faulty organisation have been guarded against by wise measures, which is not in my province here to touch upon. To the Christian soldier it should be a matter for grateful thankfulness, that, in the great issue raised between the followers of the Cross and those of Mahomet and the Hindoo idolater, it pleased Almighty God to give strength to our arms, courage to our hearts, and, finally, to bless our banners with victory. "There is a Providence that shapes our ends, rough hew them as we may." I will conclude with the words of Holy writ—"If God be for us, who can be against us."

* The native name for the river Ganges.

THE END.

www.ingramcontent.com/pod-product-compliance
Ingram Content Group UK Ltd.
Pitfield, Milton Keynes, MK11 3LW, UK
UKHW042000230426
12048UKWH00009B/442